ne

Always too many miles

Jean Stevens' poems have appeared in *London Magazine*, *Stand*, *The North*, *Myslexia*, *Other Poetry*, *Smoke*, *Brittle Star*, *The Frogmore Papers*, *The High Window*, *Obsessed with Pipework*, *Acumen*, *Pennine Platform*, *Poetry Wales*, *Poetry and Audience*, *Orbis*, *Elephant*, *Dream Catcher*, *Say Cheese,* and have won prizes and been highly commended in numerous competitions. Among them are the *Bridport Prize*, *The Yorkshire Post Poetry Prize* and *Wales Poetry Award,* and she has been shortlisted for The Poetry Business pamphlet competition and *The Rialto* Poetry Prize. Her poems have also been broadcast on Radio Leeds, BBC Radio 3 and Radio 4.

Her plays have been performed at Derby Playhouse, The Edinburgh Festival, Harrogate Theatre and West Yorkshire Playhouse, and her stand-up comedy script won The Polo Prize at London's Comedy Store.

As a professional actor she has credits for stage, radio, film and television.

jeanstevenspoet.co.uk

About other poetry collections by Jean Stevens

...searching, restless poems, haunted by both darkness and light
Kim Moore

Filmic and beautiful, full of warmth and drama
Kay Mellor OBE

An exciting contemporary voice
Daljit Nagra

Persuasive and deeply moving
The Yorkshire Times

A sure hand
Ian McMillan

For Jean Stevens, love, grief, elegy, longing are insuperable states of mind, as natural as the taking of measured breaths
Steve Whitaker

Also by Jean Stevens

Poetry

Performances (Pica Press 1999)
Undressing in Winter (Matador 2008)
Beyond Satnav (Indigo Dreams Publishing 2016)
Driving in the Dark (Naked Eye Publishing 2018)
Speak to the Earth (Naked Eye Publishing 2019)
Nothing But Words (Naked Eye Publishing 2020)

Plays

Twockers, Knockers and Elsie Smith (1997)
Journey (1998)
both published by Smith and Kraus, USA

ALWAYS TOO MANY MILES

Jean Stevens

Naked Eye Publishing

Book design and typesetting by Naked Eye

ISBN: 9781910981191

www.nakedeyepublishing.co.uk

Acknowledgements

Some of these poems were first published in *Brittle Star*, *Dream Catcher*, *Frogmore Papers*, *The North, Obsessed with Pipework*, *Pennine Platform* and *Smoke*.

The poem *Distances* was Highly Commended for the 2021 Wales Poetry Award and published in their online booklet and in *Poetry Wales.*

Perhaps being old is having lighted rooms
Inside your head, and people in them, acting
People you know, yet can't quite name.

Philip Larkin from *'The Old Fools'*

Contents

I Threshold

II The Edge of the Sands

III *Those you knew*

IV *Other Lives*

I

Threshold

Quiet

settles over the garden as if the world's
asleep, snow halfway up our boots
our breath frosting the bending trees
the creak of ice on the pond
the give of its movement
as, crossing over the water,
come the ghosts of mothers and fathers
of children and grandchildren
blending past and future to share
in the present breaking of silence.

The last time I saw you
for my daughter Alison

Evening still full of the day's heat,
we sit on your high balcony
in the canopy of rainforest trees
watch sulphur-crested cockatoos
and rainbow lorikeets commandeer the space.
We raise our wine glasses
to the overflowing day we've spent
in the heart of this city,
Botanical Gardens with desert roses,
lilies the size of dinner plates,
the blue smell of eucalypts;

the sheen on the Opera House curves,
Circular Quay's bustle of ferries
the boom of didgeridoos, the swirls
of yellow and green as acrobats
dare-devil on the waterfront;
the smell of coffee outdoors
in the sun, the ooze in our mouths
of melon, pineapple, mangoes,
as two crimson rosellas swoop
and attack the sugar bowl.

Knowing I may never see you again,
touch you again, I'm deep in how
it was then, there in that evening
the other side of the world,
as we watched the sun quickly sink,
closed down the parasols
and turned to go inside.

Distances

When we parted at Sydney Airport,
I couldn't stop myself turning
for one last look as you walked away.
Your shoulders were hunched
and I saw them shake. You became smaller and smaller
vanished through the sliding exit door.

All the times I visited you, my stay
had a little shadow in each day's sun
knowing this moment would come.

This year, plane booked, itinerary sorted,
you were going to fly back to me here
become clearer and clearer
until I could actually touch you.

But now there are rules we can't break
borders we're not allowed to cross.
I don't know how much time I've left
and whenever I think of the turning earth
I think of your sun and my moon,
my sun and your moon,
out in the endless distance of space.

When I carried you inside my body,
when I held your hand, wiped your tears,
I thought of your growing up
thought of your leaving home.
I never stopped to calculate how far
you might move away from me.
I didn't know then the tyranny of distance.

The running child

Watching TV, I travelled the Ho Chi Minh trail
and fell for the place. I wanted our next trip
to be to the lush hills and jungles,
the multiple cascades of Ban Gioc Falls,
the Golden Bridge held in the air
by two giant stone hands, and to witness
a beauty once thought to be gone forever.

Vietnam with its piles of dead, its painful,
torn history, its forests and greenery
turned to ashes by chemical warfare.
And, bombed by napalm, the running child
scorched out of her clothes. But dark days here
mean we might never travel again, or meet
in that place and see that recovery is possible.

Going back

His own children are now as far removed from him as he from
    me
yet there's no untying the worry knot. After his divorce
I saw him take a broken bottle to his wrists (not the first time

I'd held my breath). Watched him as a young man hit a tree,
overturn, hang upside down in the roll cage of his rally car.
Got the phone call: climbing with the lads, he'd injured his leg.

Heard about the drinks and smokes passed round at junior
    school.
On his fourth birthday yanked him free as he pedalled his toy
    car
down a honking road and a truck screeched towards us.

Grabbed him at six months sliding head first from a bench
towards a concrete path. Panted and pushed to get him into the
    world.
Hoped through the sickness, loss of blood, and all the other
    scares.

And, when the phone rings unexpectedly, my heart still
    acrobats.

At half past nine his heart will stop

Here he is age five, posing
in front of a snowman,
red wellies and anorak vivid
against the white, a gap-toothed
grin making a lantern of his face.

And here at ten, all legs and arms,
in his Leeds United football shirt
on a wild Northumberland beach
his racquet a blur racing through the air
as he attacks a shuttlecock.

At sixteen, hands thrust in pockets,
tight jeans, leather jacket,
shiny Ford logo on his belt,
he leans on a scarlet Capri.

Today at half past nine
he's prone on an operating table.
Doctors are stopping his heart
hoping to shock him back to life.

After his father died

There were the hymns
  the choir, the mourners, flowers.

There were the letters
  the presents, cards, calls.

There was the doctor
  the advice, the pills.

Back in the staff room
  there were the touches on the shoulder,

there was the headmistress
  who slid silently past him

then the troubled, truanting girl
  running up to him:

Sir, sir, I'm sorry, sir.
  It's shite, innit?

Threshold

As I fall asleep, I feel the sun
on my face, the hint of a breeze
shifting my hair and I'm back
on our trek again when we walked
mile after mile every day
and thought nothing of it.

I don't remember where we were
or the names of those I was with
but I smell the heat, feel the blisters,
hear the laughter of my friends.

Here's the stinging presence
of wild garlic and nettle
the puckering taste of blackberries
not really ripe enough to be picked.

Here's the hill with its purple carpet,
and slopes that go on forever,
here's the river that cooled our limbs,
the waterfall that pelted our backs.

Here's the heron still as a statue
poised between water, earth and air,
that liminal bird on the threshold of everything.
And look, who is this girl running
towards me out of the past?

Mee-maw

The noise in a weaving shed made speech impossible. Weavers
communicated by mee-mawing – exaggerated movements of the
mouth, a cross between mime and lip reading.

All the way back from now
I move unseen through the main street
of my childhood's Lancashire town
with its mee-maw messages
its clattering looms

and catch up with my father
walking through a morning still dark
and the streets unaired
try not to think about
his noisy backaching work
in a windowless garage.

I want to think about the times
out on the moors with him
grass under our feet
and breathing fresher air
when neither of us spoke except, perhaps,
a word to the dog.

I want to say the things I would have said then
if talking had been his thing.
In my pocket I have the letter he wrote
when I was about to be married
and move carelessly
into a life with someone else.

The letter I imagine him struggling with
- he had to leave school aged eleven -
the slow careful forming of words.
If he'd written volumes he couldn't have said more.

The wireless

Kathleen Ferrier on the wireless.
It's my father's way of getting close.
I hold my breath to listen.

When he mended a puncture
on my bike or hammered nails
into the sledge he made for me

or when his calloused fingers
wrestled with the tiny furniture
of the doll's house I keep to this day

he'd be humming a song
and I'd remember the lyrics
that went with the music

knowing that darling and love
had to be said by someone else
for a man of so few words.

Sprinter
for my father

You should have been
bent over at the starting line
in the latest spiked shoes.
You should have been attuned
to the jolt of the starting pistol
ready to test those legs against the world.

You should have tackled
long distance, too, had all the skills,
taught me to run across hard sand,
learning when to take a breath, when to hold
yourself back, when to give it all you've got.

You should have been a Christie or a Jackson
not lying under lorries on a cold concrete floor
and damaging your back.

We should have been shouting you on,
standing on tiptoe, hoarse with our cheers,
hoping when the race was won
you'd raise your fist in the air,
and we'd drape a flag round your shoulders
and celebrate that the world
had learned of your greatness
when you hit that finishing tape.

Monopoly

A coal fire
green baize card table
my father
the wheelbarrow.

Play:
some of us grabbed the dice
piled houses on important squares
stacked and counted cash.
Dad had to be persuaded
to buy Mayfair.

I landed on his property:
I can't ask our Jean for rent.

We could never get him
to play again.

Snow goose

She'd never been abroad. It wasn't something
people did, but later she had the chance
to go to Norway with a friend.
Her usual stiff manner disguised apprehension.

When she came back, she had a present for me.
From her tight face I knew it mattered
for me to like it. Till then I'd been the one
trying so hard to please her.

I peeled off the wrapping and saw
a beautiful snow goose carved in oak. She was
talking fast, *Couldn't find anything, had to
shop in duty free, hope it's okay.*

The tip of the beak had snapped
leaving a raw jagged edge.
Her shoulders drooped, her eyes clouded over.
It's all right I said *we can mend it.
Mum, we can mend it.*

Seen from afar

At the end of the garden,
behind a bed of red roses,
my mother hangs out the weekly wash
on the line between lichened trees.
A series of signalling flags,
pillowcases and shirts surrender
to the pouring wind: pants, blouses, petticoats
stealing the shape of breasts, thighs, bodies, dancing.
A sudden calm sucks out the air -
the clothes hang motionless on the line.

The clothes hang motionless. On the line
a sudden calm sucks out the air
stealing the shape of breasts, thighs, bodies, dancing
to the pouring wind. Pants, blouses, petticoats,
pillowcases and shirts, surrender
- a series of signalling flags.
On the line between lichened trees
my mother hangs out the weekly wash
behind a bed of red roses
at the end of the garden.

These hills
i.m. G.P.Stevens

Midnight, the longest day of the year
and already we've begun
to move back towards the dark,
but when I look out to the hills
it's still light enough to see
the climbing drystone walls,
the white dots of sheep,
a faint moon waiting to show itself.

Later the kids will text,
remembering it's your birthday,
and I wonder what I can give you.
When you were here you never
asked for, or seemed to want
anything more than you already had.

But you never saw this view
from my new cottage,
so I'm sending you these hills,
these drystone walls,
these drowsy sheep
and the ever changing moon.

Haunting

When the dark is pushed to the edges
and you get up in the morning,
I'm the splash of water in the shower
the gurgle down the plughole.

I'm the twinkle of light in your mirror
the taste of your coffee and toast
behind the words of every voice
coming from your radio.

I draw pictures in the dust -
see where my fingers have played
on surfaces like a piano, written
a different tune in every room

and, like in the music you listen to,
I'm there in the clash of cymbals
the filigree of flutes, the rise
into air of cello and double bass.

I'm in the cotton of your curtains,
the coolness of your clean sheets
in the hug of your padded overcoat
the comfort of your blanket.

I float around in your garden,
polish a leaf here and there,
I'm in the squeak of your mower
in the sand when you dress the lawn.

If you think you see and hear me
it's not because I want to scare you
it's because you're looking for ways
to make things whole again.

II

The Edge of the Sands

Locked

These locked-in days
I want to tell you how I feel

but right outside
my window are cranesbills,

geranium magnificum, and my eyes
are drawn to their vivid blue.

Within each blossom, five petals overlap
and every heart-shaped petal,

tiny as a newborn's fingernail,
has miniature stripes in deeper blue

which lead the bees
to its midnight-purple eye,

to pollen yellow as the glow
of last night's supermoon

and, as the sun retreats
behind cloud, I see

it's the flowers themselves
that hold the light.

2021

I'm in the bathroom upside down
trying to reach the loo.
She's in a helicopter looking for forest fires.
Others are being fed grapes in the land of milk and honey
pushing the world to hell.
Get yourself back, get yourself home,
there's a queue of ghosts waiting
along with a judge and jury frowning, frowning.
But next to you is Marilyn, Marilyn Monroe.
Seen it all she drawls
Most of it's shit.
There's a sense of peaceful armies forming
in upside downside sideways here.
Tigers and jaguars take up positions in the aisles.
They know they're superior.
Out of a cloud steps a woman
her hair a halo of red.
She stretches her arms to heaven. She's going to save us all.
But the rich are clutching dollar bills, stashing their bullion,
bullying, bullying bullion.
There's nothing so hard and so heavy as an ingot of gold.

Upside down

This morning
the sky's still red
fields blue, clouds yellow,
birds fly upside down,
sheep cling sideways
to drystone walls.

I fling clothes out of the wardrobe,
the cupboards, the laundry basket,
no sign of the colour I'm looking for.
Once more I dress in black.

Life has become a hunt for green -
something must still have chlorophyll
or whatever it is that fuses life
through grass and leaves.

My eyes prickle, my mind buzzes.
We were taught dozens of greens.
Now I can't even find one.
I need a child to guide me.

The edge of the sands

As day slides into evening
I walk seawards over the dunes.
A single swallow shows the way.
The horizon is far ahead,
the only sound my breath
as I feel the sting of salt in the air.

On the edge of the sands
there's a house, well-worn
but solid stone and slate.
There's no electricity
and water will have to be carried.
All the same I want to be there.

The swallow flies far ahead
and far above but when it fades
to a shadow in the distance
it turns and comes back
as if it remembers I need a guide.

I've never been to this house
but know it's waiting for me
always mere yards away
always too many miles.

Market place

The pre-dawn promise of light
the chill of a day not begun.
No stalls. No people. No traffic.
No sheep being sheared for the crowds.

A dog trots out of the shadows
seems to know where he's going.
I let him take me for a walk.
We go over the bridge down to the river
I see now he's a black and white collie,
maybe he's lost his flock.

We walk along the river bank
where rabbits you only see this early
play in the fields, and blackbirds
and wrens continue the song
begun by a robin in the night.

The lifting sun, the river's flow,
the tick-tock of time, the absorption
of creatures in the nitty-gritty of life,
and humankind irrelevant.

Scott Park

Dawn and a chill to the day. But the park's open,
the town already awake. The faint echo of engines starting,
the whistles of paperboys, the click of the letterbox.

I walk to the top of the slope where laburnums form a bridal
   arch.
Whoosh, a greyhound streaks ahead of his chubby owner
who halts and doubles over, taking great shudders of air.

The changing rooms of the tennis courts are still there,
dilapidated, crumbling into the ground.
Once full of flashes of white, rapid racquets,

and the shouts of my closest friends,
the courts have lost the game with lichen and weeds.
Nets lie torn and tangled where white lines shone.

I'd like to go in and stand where I once stood
but as I get nearer I see the path is buried
under nettles, and there's a padlock on the gate.

The furthest crag

This patch was laid with strips of turf
which over time grew to a lawn.

Though it's small, it seems as one
with the fields and craggy hills beyond.

It's been enriched by worms,
nourished by sun and rain,

here blackbirds have found their food,
my bare feet have felt its touch

but one day, when the first cowslips
bloom here and across the fields,

I shall cut a mature strip of grass
from just where I lie in the sun

until I can roll it up once more
as it was when it first arrived

and will hold it tight in my arms
instead of my daily baggage.

I'll walk slowly into the wild
and up to the top of the hill.

I will haul this living
carpet up to the furthest crag

lie down on it and close my eyes
till we both are part of the ancient turf.

The day I die
after Frank O'Hara

I've come to you late, Frank, and grieve
that all those days when I might have been
in cafés adding brandy to the coffee
while discussing Mallarmé,
I spent travelling the No 2
to work, to home, to work, to home,
leave at 8.01 get back at 17.42.

But there were snatched lunches
when I'd be in the local gallery
wrapped up in Paul Klee or Henry Moore,
or listening to a 40 minute string quartet
at Leeds Town Hall

and there were days when I walked up
the pillared steps between the lions
and the sun at a certain slant
warmed their manes and lit their eyes
as they lifted me into those other worlds.

After that crash on Fire Island beach
you died in 1966, and I'm dazed
you did so much but were only half my age.
I'm no longer thinking days or weeks or months
still trying to get my shit together counting in decades.

And I don't know why you would do it but, hey,
I just have a feeling you might
when that moment reaches my heart,
wherever you are in the ether Frank
please, stop all the clocks for me.

Companion

When the surgeon carved into my chest and inserted
you, I knew I would always have a companion.

Closer to me than anyone else has ever been,
you're mostly calm, with only a lurch now and then.

Enjoy the tentative walks I take, enjoy the taking of air,
and help me to climb the difficult hill.

Be open to the world's energy,
enjoy the sun, welcome the rain, see the beauty in snow.

Companion, show a lasting friendship,
break bread with me, take wine blessed at the altar.

Enjoy the beat of poetry, the pace of thrilling prose,
the regular tick of a clock,

take your place in the orchestra, make music
that runs from bass to descant, music that lifts the heart.

Roskilde museum

They have the skeletons
of Viking longships sunk to block the harbour
and keep the enemy out of Denmark.
Visitors learn ancient shipbuilding,
touch the bones of history.
One ship's been restored. You can sit
where the crew sat centuries ago,
wear a Viking helmet, wield the mighty oars.
That's what tourists do.

I'll sink in earth in a wild field
and rooted in my skeleton a hawthorn tree will grow.
Under the wing of Pen-y-Ghent,
Rathmell's a place without stone or wreath.
Bird feeders hang in the trees, wild flowers flourish
where children play, learn which birds to spot.
There'll be footsteps over my bones
and the sound of children laughing.
That's what children do.

Pendle Hill

Swooping sparrowhawks feel like a storm
above my head. Down there, where I set off,
the bridge seems tiny, a pen across an inkwell.

Bits of bicycle are stuck in the gorse
the kind of gorse that will always be there
ready to spring a trap for your feet.

The grass has an air of weariness, tired of pushing
back against boots and pumped-up wheels.

The air is still, clouds hang in a soft sky,
and the place fills with pictures of picnics long ago,
ricochets with laughter from boisterous kids.

This is also the place where they tested bombs
and two of my friends picked up unexploded
grenades which cost them their lives.

It's all here on Pendle Hill
along with the witches rolled down the slopes
in barrels, because they knew too much.

There are the ruins of war, the ruins of peace,
the jumbled bones of the lives we used to live.

Did you hover over my cot?

I barely gave you a thought
but I guess you always knew me.
Did you greet me in the womb
hover over my cot
hide in my satchel to go to school?

I had other things to do
dens to build, worlds to explore,
girls to share secrets, boys to flirt with,
forbidden cigarettes, and fumbling
in the back seats of the Roxy cinema.

Living away from home,
staying up late full of hope
thinking we could find answers.
Travel came next, journeys
into other people's lives.

I did think of you later on flights
when aeroplane engines stuttered.
In places that felt holy – the Palace
at Petra, Mount Fuji, the Taj Mahal.
And you drew near in the Cuban crisis,
experiments with the bomb.

Nearer again when anaesthetics
took me to a darker place
and scalpels cut my flesh.

Now I fear you've moved in,
want me to see you as familiar.
You're in every operation scar,
and attached to my ticking heart.

Leaking boat

I wake once more
feeling as if I'm a leaking boat
trying to steady myself
to the sound of pipework rattling
the smell of coconut cream shampoo
the touch of fresh-washed clothes

hoping to be one with
the morning song of unwitting birds
tick of the clock
buzz of the kettle
tang of marmalade
sun in my face
fields and hills feeding my eyes

and if the wind grows fierce,
as it recently did, I hope to be ready
to go outside and embrace it,
to love every gust, every drop of rain.

Don't let anything be drowned.
Hold on to this day.

Blank screen

That year, when The Beatles were more popular than Jesus,
we travelled by hovercraft, saw the first Action Man,
read *Wide Sargasso Sea*, goggled at *Star Trek*,
were shocked by *Cathy Come Home*.
In London: Carnaby Street, the Krays. George Blake
escaped from Wormwood Scrubs, surfaced again in Moscow.
Alf Ramsey, Moore, and the lads made the dream
come true, not knowing dementia lurked on the bench.

That year, in October, I got up to watch evening TV
soon after our baby was born. I held her
in the fiercest grip while I stared at a blank screen,
and heard there would be no programmes that night
as in Aberfan they were trawling through the mud
of a moving slag heap to find their buried children.

Muezzin

In Aqaba, Bride of the Red Sea,
with its views of Egypt and Israel,
we dived down to the greens, pinks,
blues and whites of the coral gardens,
swam with Crown Butterflies,
Golden Trevallies and Lyretails.

We squeezed through the siq's dark
eye of a needle into the light
of Petra, transported when we saw
the ancient treasury built into the cliff,
the amphitheatre and temples,
climbed to the mountain monastery.

Before dawn the next morning, chants
from the old minaret filled the air, and rolled
back the night. There was mystery
and longing in the ancient call to prayer
that made us believe it possible
nothing separates us from the other side.

Breakfast

It's a ritual now or perhaps a superstitious habit,
porridge must be stirred in one direction only,
coffee left to brew until it's time to break
the crust, stir the grains, plunge the plunger.
What has turned pleasure to duty?
When did anxiety come to live in my blood?

But this morning I'm out in the garden
in pyjamas and bare feet, talking to the beech tree,
facing up to the blackbirds,
feeling the sun come slowly out of the clouds
and hoping the freshening breeze will break
the crust holding my heart to ransom.

Buried

When you buried the teddy in the back garden
it was so it could be dug up again
when no-one was looking
but then came the unexpected new house
and, in a series of vans and cars,
over time the family moved you further away.

Years later you visited the old house
and stood outside daring yourself to knock
but how could you stand on the doorstep
and explain yourself to a stranger
when you can't explain yourself to you?

When you pressed the teddy's middle
it grunted a message over and over
and you imagine that one day
there'll be the upheaval of piles of soil
as it breaks through the earth with a roar
and becomes a bear on the prowl.

If she still had the car

she'd go for the kind of drive they did as teenagers,

turn left, then right, then straight, then right
till you were lost, hurtling into the unknown

revisiting lonely roads through the moors
patched with purple heather and gorse under a Lancashire sky

the off-road track through the Outback to the underground
town of White Cliffs where every room is studded with opals

Route 66 and the lure of Vegas glitter and kitsch
Caesar's Palace, The Grand Canal, in the middle of the desert

the elephant trail up to the temple,
to Agra and the golden mean of the Taj Mahal

the track alongside the sleek bullet train
under the spell of Mount Fuji's snowy peak

the volcanic journey to Rotorua, its spouting geysers,
bubbling mud, pools of every colour

the winter trail to Jukkasjärvi, its thigh-high snow,
sculpted ice hotel where we slept on reindeer skins

the gorge, the siq, the eye of a needle
to Petra, rose-red city half as old as time

then on the road with Thelma and Louise
driving right over the edge of the world.

III

Those you knew

Those you knew

There must be a place
      where it all makes sense.

A land with snow-topped mountains
      that seem impossible to reach,
            clear water in lakes and rivers,
                  seas filled with life

and glimpses of those you knew
      who might have chosen
            to tackle the summits
                  to swim or row the waves

or lie on never-mown grass
      wrapped up in books,
            or channel the music
                  of Dankworth, Elvis, Wolfgang.

Some would be chopping onions,
      carrots, parsnips
            picking wild garlic and herbs

others lying in the curve
      of a loved one's arms.

You'd revisit lives that crossed your own
      and hope that reaching the mountain top
            would, one day, be possible.

Beyond the rhododendrons

David, whenever I think of you,
I think of Sparky, your Airedale Terrier,
how he remained a pup when everyone else
was ageing, how he looked forlorn
if we forgot him when out in the garden
you let grow wild, how he was special,
didn't need long walks, didn't shed hair, vital
because you had trouble breathing.

The day we scattered the ashes, I looked
for him in the garden where two-legged creatures
raised champagne glasses even as they cried.
I walked beyond the rhododendrons
past the big reed-edge pond, its lilies
and irises, its hovering dragonflies,
found him among tangled wild berries,
his nose to the ground, going round in circles
sniffing, sniffing, sniffing.

The fickle sun

I saw you on the train.
My carriage had stopped at a station
just out of reach of the platform
and yours pulled up alongside
going the other way.

Two sheets of glass
and the fickle sun between us
reflected back and forth.
Your face became my face
and mine became yours
till I didn't know whether it was you
or I who had the green eyes.

Then your train set off
and, as you travelled past,
your features seemed pared to bone.

My train coughed into action
and I jerked forward into the future
wondering if we'd always moved
in opposite directions.

Your diary

Snow like the depths of Canada
nearly the height of the kids
and the forecast promised more.
We spent hour after hour building
the snowman of all snowmen,
sturdy, secure as an Inuit igloo.

Next morning we pulled back the curtains.
White had turned to a slushy grey.
A puddle held a soggy scarf and hat
the twig we used for a pipe,
bits of coal that were buttons,
and a carrot, sad and ridiculous.

That's how it was with your diary.
I thought I'd really discover you there
but the words meant so little
they seemed to slide off the page
and the substance of your life melted away
spilled through my chilly fingers.

1938

That year
he tore through the town on a motorbike
his mother never knew he had,
perfected his stand on the saddle
his leaps in the air over hollows
at speed for any girls who watched.

He trespassed in the landlord's
orchard, tasted unripe fruit,
crept up on rabbits and foxes,
tickled trout in the river,
and, chased by a gamekeeper,
ran laughing over the fields.

He rippled into muscle, needed hardly
any sleep, bubbled and overflowed
with urges, an animal
browned by sun, weathered by wind
that year.

North Sea

We'd left behind the letters
the documents, and any certainty.

Waves rammed the ferry
carelessly tossing it back and forth.

Ahead in the North of Jutland
lay the burial we were searching for
out of my family history.

When we got there, somewhere beneath our feet
would be my cousin's bones, his body trapped
in a Lancaster Bomber sucked into
Denmark's fenland marsh.

Behind us, a trail of the lost ones
in our lives. Two children who never
saw the light, the father who died
too soon, the husband
who walked out of the house
and never came back.

There on the ferry, wondering
whether we would survive the night,
we belonged in neither world.

Letter from the dead
Flying Officer Sid Forrester writing home in August 1943

Airborne since nine last night
I tumbled into bed at six
and have just got up at three.

Our new young engineer
relished his initiation
into the mysteries
of nocturnal flight.

A perfect night with a huge moon
left him with shining eyes
and laughter
adrenaline on the run
far too perky to rest.

We breathed words of wisdom:
without sleep, he'd be
blurred round the edges
no way to tackle a war.

So finally he went
whistling to his bed.

Though that young engineer has
slept for years inside his plane
deep in the fens of Jutland
I always think of him
as flying with the moon.

Edna on Fifth Avenue

She was the aunt I never met
but I'd heard this lass from the mill
had decided she'd live in America.

Google told me about the ship she boarded
and that she landed in New York.
Nothing online after that.

I wanted to see her as the daughter made good,
dressed in a business suit, equal to all the world.
I wanted her to come home for a holiday
to set Lancashire's streets alight.

But I knew that could never come true
for my mother had told me the family
story about this daring sister of hers.

How she'd collapsed with appendicitis
right there on the famous Fifth Avenue.
How the ambulance was called
but she was left lying where she was
after failing to show written proof
her insurance was fully paid up.

Uncle Wilf in the outback

He shoved his boots
to the bottom of his kitbag
with a few clothes, a compass,
his Swiss Army knife,
and a couple of biographies.
He had no time for fiction.

He made provision for his wife and kids,
left the house, hitched a lift to the docks
to work his way to Australia
- couldn't afford, like other travellers,
to be a Ten Pound Pom.

I think of him scrubbing
wallowing decks, tearing
his hands on slippery rope,

and, in the relentless heat
of the outback,
learning to ride a wild horse
and tangle with bolting cattle.
Wish I had more of his blood.

Rainy Monday

I think of my days in the outback
when every drop was precious.

I put on my wellies, turn up my collar,
I'm going to be at the heart of this.

I remember when the kids were small
we made a festival of rainy days.

Splash, spray, the joy of every puddle,
the delight in stomping back home

muddy and tired. Carelessly letting that
shining day drip on to the kitchen floor.

After she died

After she died Enid went on living
in the white blonde hair of her twin,
the solemn blue of her eyes,
the challenging way she looked at you
as if she was full of secrets.

She sat just in front of me at school,
eleven she was and, apart from the loss
of household pets, the first death
that took hold of my throat, and every
time I saw her twin my flesh shrank.

It was worse than being haunted
and more like being stalked.
Stalked by this frightening fickle thing.
This '*d*' this '*e*' this '*a*' this '*t*' this '*h*'
that obviously was pitiless.

Shirley

First the whispered words of adults
then a rumour muttered from desk to desk.
Shirley – Shirley's dead. How could you be
so full of life one minute and not the next
when you were only twelve years old?

I relived what I overheard. She got on her bike
for her daily ride, looking ahead for the blossoming
trees. She was always the first to know
spring had come, the first to pass piano exams,
the first in the poll for most popular girl.

Her front wheel caught a rut in the road
and threw her from the saddle.
She died as her head hit cat's eyes
standing proud of the ground
that winked when they caught the light.
The eyes put there to keep you safe.

Headmaster

I drift down Constable Avenue,
Reynolds Street, Alma Tadema Grove.
It's a ghost town and, back down the years,
I arrive at school and stand in the playground,
my body that of a ten-year-old
filled with the energy of the day.

In assembly I hope it's one of those days
Mr Matthews asks volunteers to come on stage
to tell everyone a story. As if at a cinema organ,
he'd sit at the piano and, for a thriller,
play in dramatic low key or, for a love story,
choose notes like a soulful violin.

In the classroom with its smell of chalk and ink
I wait through arithmetic, geography,
history, for one of Mr. Matthews' lessons
about anything he thinks will interest us.

Once he wrote on the blackboard
Manners makyth man. I felt something lift
inside me at the sight of a spelling at once
perfect and magical. He encouraged
storytelling, reading, writing, taught
me the joy of words, words, words.

The party

A gathering of children from Sunday School.
The meeting room was bright
with bunting, the tables had festive cloths.
I wore my best dress, very excited.
Parties were about enjoying yourself.

My mother, keen to rise in the social world,
had shown me how posh people
arrange their cutlery, and I practised
taking soup from a spoon directed away from me
and not slurped from the front.

Lots of my friends were around me
and the teachers served the meal.
I remember nothing about the food,
the talk or having a good time.
What I remember is taking care
I got things right when I left the table.

She swooped: *What have you forgotten?*
I stammered: *Please, miss, I put the cutlery straight
and I said please may I leave the table.*
She said: *Just look at the floor. You dropped some crumbs.*

Later in church, I watched Mrs. Johnson walk up the aisle
with her collection plate, and burned with implacable hatred.
Something inside me crossed over as I watched her
walk back to the altar, and wait to be blessed.

IV

Other Lives

Ginnel

A couple of times a week, we pass
in the ginnel, me making for the post office,
him walking the dog. A short, sturdy man,

with more shine on his head than hair,
he carries himself with shoulders back
and a lifetime of work behind him.

At first, we nodded and said *Morning*.
Then I tried him out with those British
clichés, *Nice day* or *A bit nippy*.

We know a little about each other (we live
in a very small town): the death of his son,
some problems with his wife, and he knows

of my loss, my numerous hospital trips,
and we both know *How are you?* won't do
so now he just says a cheery *Na then*.

The mother

Her hands remember
how she ran her fingers
along the thrill
of the sharpened blade

thought of soft tissue, rib cage
muscle and bone
which area would draw
unstoppable blood.

Her eyes remember
how they narrowed
her lips how they pressed tight

her brain remembers ferocity
though till then
she'd been a pacifist

but her nose remembers
the smell of milk
her arms the imprint
of the warm flesh she held

the ends of her nerves
remember the twitch of hope
she'd be able to keep them safe.

Pencil box

He'd seen how you slid
the polished lid back
to reveal crayons of every colour
that there was a hinge that swung
the opposite way into the space
for a rubber, pair of compasses,
a tiny ruler, a set square.

He imagined the feel of it
the power of knowing how it worked.

He'd heard Audrey Bottomley sniff
when she said *That boy*
smells like a dirty dishcloth.

Audrey Bottomley's dad
was the sort of dad who sat down at work.
Her mother had manicured fingers
and shoes that click-clacked down the hall
when they came to see Audrey's
Grade A course work pinned
to the classroom wall.

He threw his dirty old jacket
over his prize and scooped it up
with all the other bits and pieces
he lugged about. He didn't have a satchel.

He never used that pencil box
kept it for years
tucked away under his bed.

Bus shelter

Midnight.
The street lamps are out.

No buses, no traffic
except the battered black car
that moves slowly hugging the kerb.

A slant of moonlight
catches piles of dirt, excrement,
half-eaten food.

A cold wind shifts the lost
rotting leaves into corners.

There are cracks and holes in the grimy glass.

Then she comes.
Once there was a bench.
Now she lies, head on a torn rucksack,
in the corner least troubled by draughts.

She's still wearing men's boots,
a filthy knitted hat,
still carrying a knife.

Afterwards

She was sitting on the bench
when the man came up muttering.
His clothes were torn and stained
his toes stuck out of his grotty shoes.
That's mine. I sleep here.

Last month, last week, yesterday
she'd have been frightened
would have hastily moved away
among the joggers and keep-fit kids
the mothers and children
throwing bread to the squabbling ducks.

But now, *It's our bench* she said
It belongs to everyone.
He leant towards her, his breath
a blast of poison. She looked at the red
in his eyes. The dirt-filled creases
on his face. His weary shoulders.

We're all where you are she said.
And where's that? He was sneering.
She looked at her bitten fingernails.
I don't know she said.

Pye Black Box

I lug the old record player out of the loft
and lift its shiny black lid.
Although the vinyl has gone to the dump,
still on the turntable the B side of a single
lies ready for the arm to be swung across
the needle to be guided by a steady hand.
Maybe I didn't love you ... drifts out
of the past for fans to pick up on the breeze.

Then, crowding out of the dark,
comes a cavalcade of ghosts,
lost singers from every era and age,
and into the light come Otis, Buddy, Kurt,
Janis, Jimi, Dusty, Elvis, Amy
and all the ones who left too soon.

Scarborough

Still, the castle, the headland, the pier,
the day's motorbikes have left,
even the seagulls are sated and quiet,
only the sussuration of waves, a tide on the turn.

The sun slips over the horizon
into the shining water.
A chilling breeze
brings swirls of grey cloud.

A lone child in a yellow t-shirt
on the edge between land and sea
runs forward as the waves shrink away
slides back as they come for his feet,

a dance with rhythms of forward and back
in balance with the movements of earth,
developing the grace of an acrobat
and learning to work with nature.

From this room
for Ian

At the back in my garden
there's brilliance in the air
and, though the rowan persists in greens,
autumn paints the hillside red, copper, bronze,
blackbirds rummage through leaves
and a wren flies boldly
from the gap in the drystone wall.

At the front, passing me by,
beyond clusters of hanging-on roses
are glimpses of other lives.
And flashes of sun on windscreens
give parked cars an air of impatience
as if they're stamping their hooves
ready to power into life.

The coming of the dark

brings with it the light of other lives,
yellow warmth trickling through the trees
from the farm on the hill,

the intensity of arc lights
on shouting children
rolling in mud and learning
the rules of the game.

Hints of a clouded moon.
The blues of an emergency.
The bright or dipped shafts
of leaving cars and motorbikes

driving forward on their own beams
and looking ahead for the light
that will bring them home.

Naked Eye Publishing

A fresh approach

Naked Eye Publishing is five years in existence and still fledgling: an independent not-for-profit micro-press intent on publishing quality poetry and literature, including in translation. We are also developing a 'Potted Theses' series: academic theses rewritten for the general reader.

A particular focus is translation. We aim to take a midwife role in facilitating the translation of works that have until now been disregarded by English-language publishing. We will be happy if we function purely as an initial stepping-stone both for overlooked writers and first-time literary translators.

Each of us at Naked Eye is a volunteer, competent and professional in our work practice, and not intending to make a profit for the press. We see ourselves as part of the revolution in book publishing, embodying the newly levelled playing field, sidestepping the publishing establishment to produce beautiful books at an affordable price with writers gaining maximum benefit from sales.

nakedeyepublishing.co.uk

Lightning Source UK Ltd.
Milton Keynes UK
UKHW020756210322
400370UK00007B/137